STARTERS
PLACES

Australia

Macdonald Educational

About Starters Places

Starters Places provide an entertaining and informative introduction for young children to various countries and their national characteristics.

The vocabulary is controlled for reading by young children, and about 90 per cent of the words in the book should be familiar to young readers.

Each book contains material for further activities and research, such as an easy reference map, a table of simple facts, a project, a dictionary and an index.

Teachers and experts have been consulted on the content and accuracy of the books.

Illustrated by: Ionicus

Written and planned by: Jennifer Vaughan

Art consultant: Geoffrey Dickinson of Punch

Reading consultant: Donald Moyle, author of The Teaching of Reading and senior lecturer in education at Edge Hill College of Education

Teacher panel: Frank Blackwell, Loveday Harmer, Lynda Snowdon, Joy West, Enid Wilkinson

Colour reproduction by
Colourcraftsmen Limited

Filmset by
Layton-Sun Limited

© Macdonald Educational
Limited 1973
Fourth impression 1976
Made and printed in Great Britain
by Hazell, Watson & Viney Limited
Aylesbury, Buckinghamshire

ISBN 0 356 04232 4
First published 1973 by
Macdonald Educational Limited
Holywell House
Worship Street
London EC2

opera house

Sydney is a city in Australia.
It has a big harbour
and a new opera house.

The weather is often hot.
People like to go surfing.

These people are in
a glass bottomed boat.
They are looking at coral
on the Great Barrier Reef.

Australians drink
cold beer in summer.
Many people like to swim.
4

commentator

cameraman

These people are watching cricket.
This is a Test Match.
The Australians are playing England.

These men are hunting crocodiles.
Crocodile skin
is used for handbags and shoes.

Much of Australia is desert.
There is a big rock
in the desert.
It is called Ayer's rock.

sacred dance

digeridoo

Here are some Aborigines.
They live in the outback,
away from the towns.

8

boomerang

spears

Aborigines lived in Australia
long before anyone else came.
They use boomerangs to hunt with.

miner

There are mines in the desert.
Men earn a lot of money
mining for nickel.
Nickel is a kind of metal.

10

Inside the space station

This space station is in Australia.
The first pictures from the moon
were received here.

This dam is in the mountains.
It stores water.
There are power stations here.

12

People can ski
on the mountain sides in winter.
It is winter in Australia
when it is summer in Britain.

The weather in Australia
is good for growing fruit.
Oranges, apples and pineapples
all grow in Australia.

14

Australian farms are called homesteads.
This man is a stockman.
He rounds up the sheep
and drives them to the homestead.

The wool is being
clipped off the sheep.
This is called shearing.
Wool is used to make cloth.

teacher

The children on a homestead
are a long way from school.
They have their lessons by radio.

Someone on this homestead is ill.
The doctor comes in an aeroplane.
He is called the Flying Doctor.

18

These children live in a town.
They are at the zoo.
There are all kinds of Australian animals
at the zoo.

Australia long ago

Long ago
Captain Cook came to Australia.
His ship sailed
into Botany Bay.

The British sent
many prisoners to Australia.
They were sent in old ships.
These were called hulks.

At first everyone lived
by the sea.
Then men discovered
rich lands beyond the mountains.

22

Gold was found in Australia.
People came from all over the world
to look for gold.

23

Ned Kelly was a bushranger.
A bushranger was an Australian bandit.
Ned Kelly wore armour
to save him from bullets.

Make yourself some armour
like Ned Kelly's.
Use cardboard and sticky tape.

Index

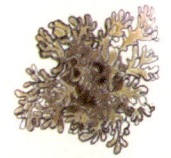

Facts about **Australia**

Population: 13,500,000

Federal capital: Canberra

State capitals: Sydney, Melbourne, Brisbane, Perth, Adelaide, Hobart

Main ports: Fremantle, Melbourne, Sydney, Adelaide, Brisbane

Currency: Australian dollars and cents

National airlines: Qantas, Trans Australia Airlines, Ansett Airlines

Highest mountain: Mount Kosciusko (7,300 feet)

Main rivers: Murray, Darling, Murrumbidgee

Average summer temperature:
Melbourne 20°C, Darwin 32°C

Average winter temperature:
Melbourne 10°C, Darwin 24°C

Popular sports: Four kinds of football, tennis, cricket, skiing, surfing

Main products: Wheat, wool, beef, lamb, butter, cheese, steel, aluminium, nickel